Once it has been spoken...

...It cannot be unspoken

Kutiikiitowaakanun

kuh-tee-key-toe-WOK-in-un

Our Nanticoke Language

Written by Keith Cunningham, Karelle Hall, and RagghiRain

Illustrations by Paige McNatt

Photographs by Fred Shaw

For more information about the Nanticoke Language Project, please check out our website at www.nanticokelanguage.org

Copyright © 2023 by Keith Cunningham, Karelle Hall, and RagghiRain

All rights reserved. No part of this book may be reproduced or reprinted without the direct written consent of the authors.

ISBN 978-1-62806-371-4 (print | paperback)

Library of Congress Control Number 2023903309

Published by Salt Water Media
29 Broad Street, Suite 104
Berlin, MD 21811
www.saltwatermedia.com

All illustrations are by Paige McNatt and used with permission.

All photographs are by Fred Shaw - unless otherwise noted in the caption - and are used with permission.

For more information about the Nanticoke Language Project, please check out our website at www.nanticokelanguage.org

Kutiikiitowaakanun

kuh-tee-key-toe-WOK-in-un

Our Nanticoke Language

Audio Recorded in Red Blanket
Entertainment LLC Studio
Bridgeton, NJ

Speakers:
Keith Cunningham
Karelle Hall
Herman Jackson
RagghiRain
Cory Ridgeway
Urie Ridgeway

Mat Haashii
Written by: RagghiRain
Performed by: Red Blanket Singers

Language Project Partner:
Jennifer Kerby

Dedication

To write a simple acknowledgment and speak words of gratitude to all involved? There is no way!

Little Brother Duane Johnson and Little Sister Doris Johnson invited Dr. Bonnie Hall and me to go through and read the information in boxes of the essential works of Jean Princess Laughing Water Norwood. We each had stacks of folders and would share the folders we believed needed to be marked and set aside.

Little Brother and Bonnie were sharing a folder, and a small discussion was happening as Doris and I continued to work. I heard my name and looked up. Little Brother simply said, "Jean left this behind for you." I opened the folder to find her detailed journal of the Nanticoke Language Project and a list of Tribal and Community Members supporting the work. These were the Ones determined to breathe life into the Nanticoke Language. In honor of those who began the journey in 2006, we are recording their names here so you will know them and remember them: Chief Tee Norwood, Jean Norwood, Pecita Lonewolf, Odette Wright, Sharkey Wright, William Davis, Sylvia Pinkett, Barbara Jackson, Joan Ridolfi, Dottie LaCates, Rev. Roy Bundy, Sterling Street, and Myrelene Ranville (Anishinaabe of Canada and speaker of a sister language). Jean had written a title she hoped to have on the book: "Then I'll Leave This Life Having Heard My Language." May we all memorize these words.

For the last three years, tears of joy and tears of struggle have flowed as Jean continually reminds us and pushes us hard from the place beyond. The Language Project Family wants to thank everyone who has supported this work and believed in the vision. Because...

"Then We'll Leave This Life having Heard Our Language."

November 2006/June 2023

Nanticoke Language Project Family

Message from Our Linguist

Dear Relatives,

It brings me great joy to present to you what will be the first of many textual resources to revitalize the Nanticoke language. It is a product of years of research and collaboration between me and members of your community. However, you, dear reader, are the most important factor in the success of our revitalization movement. The lessons contained in this book provide a new voice for words spoken by your ancestors more than two centuries ago. It is your birthright as Nanticoke people to reclaim these words from archived documents and bring them home to be part of your daily life. The language may seem foreign and daunting at first from the perspective of an English speaker. However, it is my hope that regular study will make it seem more like a relative returning home after a long absence. Importantly, do not fear making mistakes and do not feel that there is a single correct way of speaking. While English discourse is artificially governed by a myriad of artificial prescriptive rules, your ancestors' speech allowed for more variety. Just as we have unique personalities, our ways of speaking differ in subtle ways that reflect our individuality.

I would like to thank my colleagues Karelle Hall, Ragghi Rain, Paige McNatt, Reverend Jennifer Kerby, and Reverend Fred Shaw for making this work possible. I would also like to thank Sterling Street for his encouragement of my work over the years. I am also grateful to Raymond Whritenour for graciously providing me with advice on grammar based upon his 40 years of research on Mission Delaware. I would also like to thank Dr. Conor Quinn for his input on the grammar of introductory phrases and the phonology of kinship terms and animal names. I am also grateful to my advisor, Dr. Lourdes Ortega for her guidance and support over the years. Finally, I would like to dedicate this work to the memory of my friends the late Seiko Shields and the late Reverend James Shields. Shields-sensei inspired my love for languages, as well as teaching me the importance of language for understanding and embracing the perspectives of people of various backgrounds. Shields-sensei truly set me on a good path in life, and my work with the Nanticoke language is inspired to a large degree by the quest for understanding that Shields-Sensei imparted to me. Reverend Shields was a pillar of his community, who organized an inclusive congregation long before it was commonplace. He and Seiko truly lived a life of love as the Apostle Paul exhorted us to do.

Keith Cunningham

Table of Contents

It Is Good To See You My Friend 1

Tecumseh Prayer 2

Importance of Language Revitalization 4

Greetings 9

Family 11

Counting 20

Animals 22

Colors and Animacy 28

    Animate Colors 29

    Inanimate Colors 38

Seven Sacred Directions 47

Body Parts 50

Let's Eat 53

Natural World 58

Powwow 65

    Drumbeat 70

Giveaway 74

Mat Haashi (Never Again) 75

Wuliikun naawul niitaap
Wu-LEE-kun   NAH-wul   NEE-tahp
(It is good to see you my friend.)

Wuliikun naawuleekw niitaapeetookw
wu-LEE-kun   NAH-wuh-lay-kw   nee-tah-PAY-toke
(It is good to see you my friends.)

Tecumseh Prayer

Eentaa weshpaakee toohkiishanee,
EHN-tah   wesh-pah-KAY   toe-KEY-sha-nay
"When you arise in the morning,

    keenaamwish wunchii waapanee,
    key-NAHM-wish   WUNT-chee   WAH-paw-nay
    give thanks for the morning light,

        kiikwaak, waak miskisuwaak.
        keek-WOK   wok   miss-kiss-su-WOK
        for your life and strength.

            Keenaamwish wunchii miitsuwaak
            key-NAHM-wish   WUNT-chee   meet-sue-WOK
            Give thanks for your food

Tecumseh Prayer cont...

waak kiikwaakanii wuleelendamuwaak.
wok   keek-WAH-ka-nee wuh-lay-len-dum-mu-WOK
and the joy of living.

    Taaku kaskii maskumoowanee
    TAH-coo KAH-ski moss-coo-MOW-wa-nay
    If you see no reason

    kwaakw weelhik keenaamuwaakanint,
    KWAH-kw   WELL-leek kay-nah-moo-WOK-kah-neent
    for giving thanks,

        na kutsaanaawsuwaak...
        nah kut-sah-nah-suh-WOK
        the fault lies with yourself..."

Importance of Language Revitalization

It is important for us to revitalize our language because it links us back to our ancestors, gives us self-esteem, especially our younger ones, enhances our culture, and strengthens our bonds to our community. It will also help to reinforce our identity. It's what makes us unique, and even prouder to be Nanticoke.

Sterling Street
Museum Coordinator
Nanticoke Indian Museum

I will be your guide on this language journey!

On each line you will see a Nanticoke word/phrase in **bold**, a phonetic pronunciation underneath in *italics*, and then the English word/phrase in parenthesis (). The capitalized section in each phonetic line shows where the stress in each word is.

For example:

Iwiinitu
ih-WEAN-ih-too
(hello/peace)

There are some sounds in Nanticoke that we don't use in English.

When you see an asterisk* after a letter in the phonetic pronunciation, it sounds a bit like a silent H or fogging glass with your breath.
For example let's look at the word for Earth:
Ahkiy
uh*-KEY

Also, when you see "kw" at the end of a word, it sounds like a whispered whoosh: *quah*; like when we say "quiet" in English.
For example let's look at the word for deer:
Atkw
UT-kw

Eelaankoomakiik
eh-lon-go-MA-keek
(All my relations/Family)

Noohkom
NOH*-come
(my grandmother)

Numuhshooms
nuh-muh*-SHOHMS
(my grandfather)

Nik
Nick
(my mother)

Noohs
Noh*s
(my father)

Our families are closely connected and we use the same words for our siblings and our cousins

Nimhs
Nihms
(my older sister/cousin)

Niimat
NEE-mut
(my older brother/cousin)

Nihsum
NIH*-sum
(my younger sibling/cousin)

We use different names for our aunts and uncles if they are on our mother's or father's side

Nikaatut
nih-KAH-tut
(my aunt/
mother's
sister)

Nsiihs
nuh-CEASE
(my uncle/
mother's
brother)

Noohtut
NOOH*-tut
(my uncle/
father's
brother)

Numiilihtakw
nuh-ME-lih*-tah-kw
(my aunt/
father's sister)

In Nanticoke, we have to change the word a bit when we talk *about* our family members and when we talk *to* them. You have just learned in the last few pages how to talk about your family. Now let me show you how to talk to them.

When I talk to my **eelaankoomakiik** (family) I add [aatii] to the end of the word.

Nik => Nikaatii
(about my mother) => (to my mother/mom)

Noohs => Noohsaatii
(about my father) => (to my father/dad)

Let's practice!

Koolamalus ha nikaatii?
co-la-MALL-us ha nih-KAH-tee?
(How are you Mom?)

or

Koolamalus ha noohsaatii?
co-la-MALL-us ha nooh*-SAH-tee?
(How are you Dad?)

Noolamalus niitsaanaatii
no-la-MALL-us nit-sa-NAH-tee
(I am well my child.)

When we talk to our grandparents we can make the word cozy like we do in English. Grandfather becomes Grandpa or Pop Pop.

Numuhshoomsaatii => Muhshoomsaatii
(Grandfather => Grandpa)

Noohkomaatii => Oomaatii
(Grandmother => Grandma)

Iwiinitu noohshiitii
ih-WEAN-ih-too no*-SHEET-tee
(Hello Grandchild)

Iwiinitu muhshoomsaatii
ih-WEAN-ih-too muh-shom-SAH-tee
(Hello Grandpa)

or

Iwiinitu oomaatii
ih-WEAN-ih-too oh-MAH-tee
(Hello Grandma)

Let's learn the words for person, man, and woman.

Iyin
EE-yin
(Person)

Naap
nahp
(Man)

Ahkwaahaak
ah*-KWA-hawk
(Woman)

Let's count the kaains!

Kaain
KAH-yeen
(corn)

Kaains
KAH-yeens
(corn - plural)

Let's count!

Nukwit
nuh-QUIT
(one)

Nukwit kaain
nuh-QUIT KAH-yeen
(one ear of corn)

Niis
neese
(two)

Niis kaains
neese KAH-yeens
(two ears of corn)

Nuhsw
nuhs
(three)

Nuhsw kaains
nuhs KAH-yeens
(three ears of corn)

Yaaw
yahw
(four)

Yaaw kaains
yahw KAH-yeens
(four ears of corn)

Nupayaa
NUH-pie-yah
(five)

Nupayaa kaains
NUH-pie-yah KAH-yeens
(five ears of corn)

Keep counting the kaains!

Nukwutaa
no-kwuh-TA
(six)

Miyaawaa
me-YAW-wah
(seven)

Tsaa
tah
(eight)

Peesukonkw
Pass-UH-con-kw
(nine)

Mitaa
mih-TA
(ten)

Animals

Let me introduce you to some of my animal friends.

When we want to talk about more than one animal we usually add **[ak]** to the end of the word to make it plural, just like the letter **[s]** in English.

For example:
Kaahaas = crow
Kaahaasak = crows

Kaahaas
KAH-hoss
(crow)

Atkw
UT-kw
(deer)

Kaahaasak
KAH-hoss-ahk
(crows)

Atkwak
UT-kwuk
(deer-plural)

The word kaahaas imitates a crow's caw and the word atkw is like the sound a deer makes.

Wiinkipim
WINK-ih-pim
(bear)

Wiinkipimiyak
wink-ih-PIM-me-ahk
(bears)

This name means "good fat" showing how bears get nice and big to prepare for winter and how important bear fat is to the Nanticoke people.

Wiinkiyooks
WIN-key-oaks
(wolf)

Wiinkiyooksak
win-KEY-oak-sahk
(wolves)

This name means "they like meat" and these furry hunters eat a lot of it!

Waapaantup
WA-pun-tup
(bald eagle)

I am named for my signature "white head"

Waapaantupeewak
wa-pun-tup-AY-wahk
(bald eagles)

Waakws
wox
(fox)

Waakwsak
WOX-suck
(foxes)

Toolup
TOLL-up
(turtle)

Toolupeewak
toll-up-PAY-wok
(turtles)

Muhkuwee
MUH*-ku-way
(squirrel)

Muhkooweewak
muh*-KO-way-wok
(squirrels)

The Living World Around Us

We use different words to talk about living, **animate** beings like you and me, and **inanimate** objects like chairs and shoes.

Our Nanticoke people recognize a world that is full of living beings. Animals, plants, the stars, water, and many more are all known to be alive, moving, or filled with spirit and we show them respect in our language by using the same terms we would use to talk about other people.

Animate and Inanimate

In English, **he**, **she**, and **they** (animate pronouns) are often only used for talking about people; example: She is tall.

In English, if we wanted to talk about an animal or a plant or a building we would use **it** (inanimate pronoun); example: It is tall.

In Nanticoke, we use animate pronouns far more often to describe the living world around us.

Animate Colors

Animate beings include humans like you, and turtles like me.
Animals, trees, flowers, and even certain foods are all animate beings!

When we talk about more than one animate being we add that same **[ak]** ending we used with the animals.

Let's look at how to talk about animate beings in different colors.

Pskwisuw (red-animate)
ps-KWISS-so

Let's practice some sentences:

wataayeesak
wa-TAH-yes-ock
(flowers)

Pskwisuwak yook
ps-KWISS-so-wok   yuk

wataayeesak
wa-TAH-yes-ock
(These flowers are red)

waakws
wox
(fox)

Pskwisuw na waakws
ps-KWISS-so   nah   wox
(That fox is red)

Wiisaawisuw (yellow-animate)
we-SOW-wiss-so

Let's practice some sentences:

psiikwuhs
ps-EE-kwus
(bird)

Wiisaawisuw wa
we-SOW-wiss-so   wah

psiikwuhs
ps-EE-kwus
(This bird is yellow)

kwaakwaams
QUOCK-quoms
(duck)

Wiisaawisuw na
we-SOW-wiss-so   nah

kwaakwaams
QUOCK-quoms
(That duck is yellow)

Askaahtukwisuw (green-animate)
ahss-kah-TUCKW-so

Let's practice some sentences:

alukwis
a-LUCK-wiss
(frog)

Askaahtukwisuw wa
ahss-kah-TUCKW-so   wah

alukwis
a-LUCK-wiss
(This frog is green)

toolup
TOLL-up
(turtle)

Askaahtukwisuw na
ahss-kah-TUCKW-so   nah

toolup
TOLL-up
(That turtle is green)

Puskweewisuw (blue-animate)
puh-SKWAY-we-so

Let's practice some sentences:

nameehs
NUH-mass
(fish)

Puskweewisuw wa
puh-SKWAY-we-so   wah

nameehs
NUH-mass
(This fish is blue)

taahkwah
TA*-quah
(crab)

Puskweewisuw na
puh-SKWAY-we-so   nah

taahkwah
TA*-quah
(That crab is blue)

Waapisuw (white-animate)
WOP-so

Let's practice some sentences:

koowaant
CO-want
(owl)

Waapisuw wa
WOP-so   wah

koowaant
CO-want
(This owl is white)

alumok
A-lum-uck
(dogs)

Waapsuwak eenuk
wop-SO-wok   EH-nuck

alumok
A-lum-uck
(Those dogs are white)

Ooskisuw (black-animate)
OHS-kso

Let's practice some sentences:

kaahaas
KAH-hoss
(crow)

Ooskisuw wa
OHS-kso   wah

kaahaas
KAH-hoss
(This crow is black)

wiinkipim
WINK-ih-pim
(bear)

Ooskisuw na
OHS-kso   nah

wiinkipim
WINK-ih-pim
(That bear is black)

Wiipunkwisuw (gray-animate)
we-PUNK-so

Let's practice some sentences:

wiinkiyooks
WIN-key-oaks
(wolf)

Wiipunkwisuw wa
we-PUNK-so   wah

wiinkiyooks
WIN-key-oaks
(This wolf is gray)

muhkuwee
MUH*-ku-way
(squirrel)

Wiipunkwisuw na
we-PUNK-so   nah

muhkuwee
MUH*-ku-way
(That squirrel is gray)

Pahsahkwiinaakwisuw (brown-animate)
puh-suck-we-KNOCK-so

Let's practice some sentences:

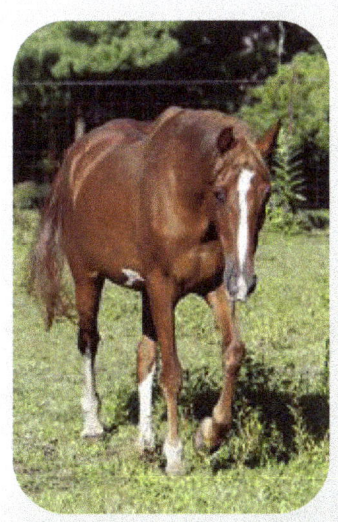

naahnaayoongus
nah*-nay-YON-gus
(horse)

Pahsahkwinaakwisuw wa
puh-suck-we-KNOCK-so   wah

naahnaayoongus
nah*nay-YON-gus

(This horse is brown)

ptukw
p-TOOK-w
(tree)

Pahsahkwinaakwisuw na
puh-suck-we-KNOCK-so   nah

ptukw
p-TOOK-w

(That tree is brown)

Inanimate Colors

Inanimate objects are things like clothes, rocks, or toys.

Let's look at how to talk about inanimate objects in different colors.

Pskweeyuw (red-inanimate)
ps-KWAY-you

Let's practice some sentences:

maalashkwists
ma-LUSH-kwiss-ts
(beans)

Pskweeyuwas yoos
ps-KWAY-you-woss   yose

maalashkwists
ma-LUSH-kwiss-ts
(These beans are red)

maskiihkwimin
muss-KEY-kwuh-min
(strawberry)

Pskweeyuw yo
ps-KWAY-you   yoh

maskiihkwimin
muss-KEY-kwuh-min
(This strawberry is red)

Wiisaaweeyuw (yellow-inanimate)
we-SAW-way-you

Let's practice some sentences:

kaain
KAH-yeen
(corn)

Wiisaaweeyuw yo
we-SAW-way-you   yoh

kaain
KAH-yeen
(This corn is yellow)

munoot
mun-OAT
(basket)

Wiisaaweeyuw nu
we-SAW-way-you   nuh

munoot
mun-OAT
(That basket is yellow)

Askaahtukweeyuw (green-inanimate)
ahss-cut-ah-KWAY-you

Let's practice some sentences:

maankwipakw
MON-kwey-pock-w
(leaf)

Askaahtukweeyuw yo
ahss-cut-ah-KWAY-you   yoh

maankwipakw
MON-kwey-pock-w
(This leaf is green)

maskoos
musk-OSE
(grasses)

Askaahtukweeyuwas
ahss-cut-ah-KWAY-you-woss

yoos maskoos
yose   musk-OSE
(These grasses are green)

Puskweeweeyuw (blue-inanimate)
puh-SKWAY-way-you

Let's practice some sentences:

ahsin
uh*-SIN
(stone)

Puskweeweeyuw yo
puh-SKWAY-way-you   yoh

ahsin
uh*-SIN
(This stone is blue)

miins
means
(berries)

Puskweeweeyuwas
puh-skway-WAY-you-wuss

yoos miins
yose   means
(These berries are blue)

Waapeeyuw (white-inanimate)
WOP-pay-you

Let's practice some sentences:

waawh
wuah
(egg)

Waapeeyuw yo
WOP-pay-you   yoh

waawh
wuah
(This egg is white)

matahkw
muh-TOCK-w
(cloud)

Waapeeyuw nu
WOP-pay-you   nuh

matahkw
muh-TOCK-w
(That cloud is white)

Ooskeeyuw (black-inanimate)
OSE-kay-you

Let's practice some sentences:

wulaak
wuh-LOCK
(bowl)

Ooskeeyuw yo
OSE-kay-you   yoh

wulaak
wuh-LOCK
(This bowl is black)

wiihskwaats
WEEH*-squats
(strands of hair)

Ooskeeyuwas yoos
ose-KAY-you-wuss   yose

wiihskwaats
WEEH*-squats
(These strands of hair are black)

Wiipunkweeyuw (gray-inanimate)
we-punk-WAY-you

Let's practice some sentences:

waapaasanee
wop-pah-SAW-nay
(blanket)

Wiipunkweeyuw yo
we-punk-WAY-you   yoh

waapaasanee
wop-pah-SAW-nay
(This blanket is gray)

punkw
PUNK-w
(ashes)

Wiipunkweeyuw yo
we-punk-WAY-you   yoh

punkw
PUNK-w
(These ashes are gray)

Pahsahkwiinaakwat (brown-inanimate)
puh-suck-we-NAH-kwhut

Let's practice some sentences:

aahpw
AH*-pw
(bread)

Pahsahkwinaakwat yo
puh-suck-we-NAH-kwhut   yoh

aahpw
AH*-pw
(This bread is brown)

mahkusuns
MOH*kuh-suns
(shoes/moccasins)

Pahsahkwinaakwahtoos
puh-suck-we-NAH-kwhut-tose

yoos mahkusuns
yose   MOH*kuh-suns
(These shoes/moccasins are brown)

Seven Sacred Directions

We recognize **Seven Sacred Directions**:

East, **South**, **West** and **North**, as well as **Above**, **Below**, and the **Center** of ourselves.

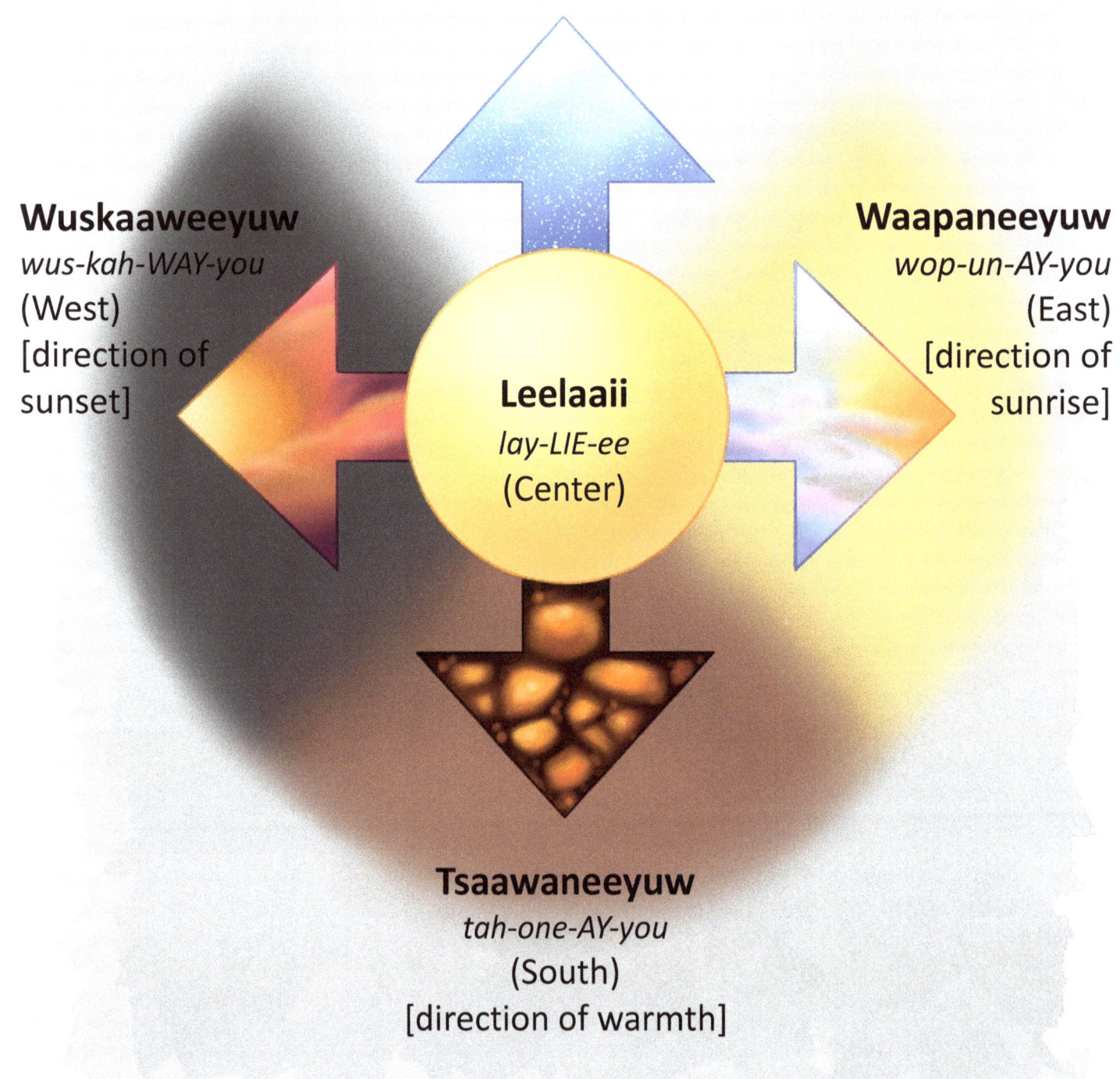

Spumint
SPUH-meent
(Above)

Aalaamii wuntaahkw
a-LA-me wuhn-TAH-kw
(Below)

Let's Name My Body Parts

Nuskiintsk
nuh-SKEENTS-k
(my eye)

Nuskiintskwas
nuh-SKEENTS-kwuss
(my eyes)

Nuhtawak
NUH*-ta-wok
(my ear)

Nihkiiw
nih*-KEY-ow
(my nose)

Nuhtawaks
NUH*-ta-woks
(my ears)

Ntoon
n-TONE
(my mouth)

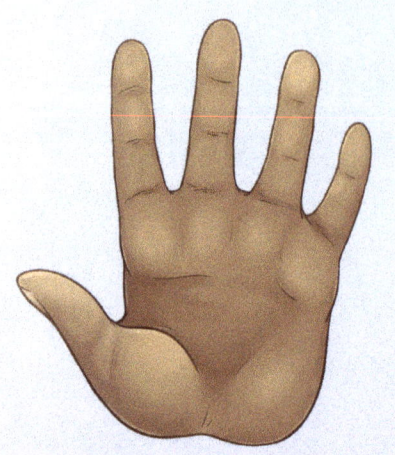

Numisiiaakwulunchum
nuh-miss-see-ock-wull-UN-chum
(my finger)

Numisiiaakwulunchums
nuh-miss-see-ock-wull-UN-chums
(my fingers)

Nulunc
nuh-LUNTS
(my hand)

Nuluncas
nuh-LUNTS-us
(my hands)

Nusiitkwaanum
nuh-SEAT-kwun-um
(my toe)

Nusiitkwaanums
nuh-SEAT-kwun-ums
(my toes)

Nist
nihst
(my foot)

Nistas
NIHS-tahs
(my feet)

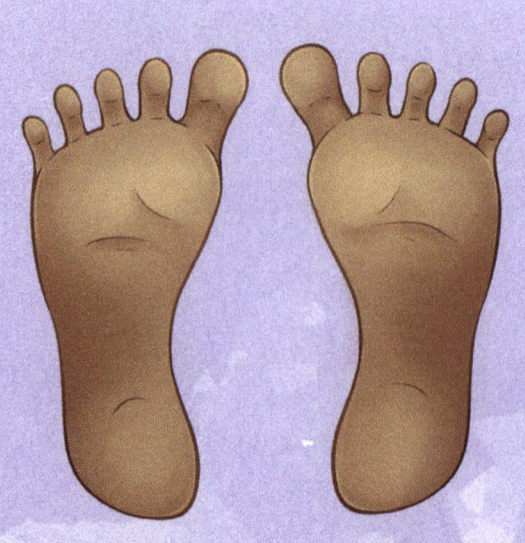

Miitsiitam! (Let's Eat!)
meet-SEE-tahm

Maalashkwists
ma-LUSH-kwiss-ts
(beans)

Kaain
KAH-yeen
(corn)

Mahkahkw
mah*-KAH*-kw
(pumpkin)

Many foods that grow in the ground, in Mother Earth, are animate like these below:

Do you see the **[ak]** plural animate ending?

Oohpun
OH*-pun
(potato)

Oohpunak
OH*-pun-ahk
(potatoes)

Pumptukwahkii ooleepun
pum-took-WAH*-key o-LAY-pun
(ramp)

Pumptukwahkii ooleepunak
pum-took-WAH*-key o-lay-PUN-ahk
(ramps)

Aahkookw
AH*-coke-kw
(mushroom)

Aahkookweewak
ah*-COKE-way-wok
(mushrooms)

Moonun
MO-nun
(clam)

Moonunak
MO-nun-ahk
(clams)

Kaahkee
KAH*-kay
(oyster)

Kaahkeewak
KAH*-kay-wok
(oysters)

Wiiyoos
we-YOSE
(meat)

Ahtukwii wiiyoos
AH*-took-we we-YOSE
(deer meat/venison)

Paahkwun
PAH*-quin
(turkey)

Paahkwunii wiiyoos
PAH*-quin-ee we-YOSE
(turkey meat)

Just like with colors, we use different words to describe how we eat animate and inanimate foods:

Moohw (to eat something animate)
MOH*-w

Miitsii (to eat something inanimate)
MEET-see

Let's Practice:

Numoohwak kaahkeewak (I eat oysters) [animate]
nuh-MOH*-wok KAH*-kay-wok

Numiitsiin kaain (I eat corn) [inanimate]
nuh-MEET-seen KAH-yeen

Our Natural World

Let's learn some words to talk about the natural world around us.

In English, we talk about weather like thunder and lightning as objects.

In Nanticoke, they are verbs or action words: to be lightning, or to be thundering.

Ahkiy
uh*-KEY
(Earth)

Ahkwahkw
ah*-KWAH-kw
(Sun)

Pumolaankwak
pum-a-LON-kwok
(Stars)

Eehtupkoonihaank
eh*-teup-CONE-ih-honk
(Moon)

Matahkw
mat-AH*-kw
(cloud)

Matahkwat
MAT-ah*-kwat
(to be a cloudy sky)

Moosahkwat
MOOSE-ah*-kwat
(to be a clear sky)

Aputaaw
A-put-ahw
(it is hot)

Kwunuk kwunuk
qun-UCK qun-UCK
(rainbow)

Eeweesh
eh-WESH
(to be wind)

Eeweeshaak
eh-WESH-ahk
(to thunder)

Saapii
SAH-pee
(to lightning/to flash)

Sookulaan
SOAK-a-lon
(to rain)

Aawan
AH-one
(fog)

Wiineew
WEAN-ay-o
(falling snow)

Koon
cone
(snow on the ground)

Ahk takwac
ahk tah-QUTZ
(ice/the ground is frozen)

Tahkeeyuw
tah*-KAY-you
(it is cold)

Siikwanuw
SEEK-one-o
(Spring)
[when the sap runs]

Meehshaak Waapanuw
meh-SHOCK   WOP-on-o
(Summer)
[when the light is great]

Wiisaapanuw
we-SAH-pawn-o
(Fall/Autumn)
[when the light is weak]

Pupoonuw
pup-OH-no
(Winter)
[when it snows]

Tunt
tunt
(fire)

Nip
nip
(water)

Mun
mun
(to drink)

Numun nip
nuh-MUN nip
(I drink water)

Powwow

A powwow is a social gathering to bring our Native communities together. We dance in remembrance of our Ancestors, for those who can no longer dance, and to welcome those who are yet unborn. We give thanks to Kiisheelumukweengw for our many blessings.

Our powwows are homecomings and intertribal gatherings. We meet new relatives from across Turtle Island. We learn and share our cultural ways, the teachings of our regalia, and so much more.

A powwow is open to the public to help educate people about our diversity and unique differences and similarities. Our cultural truths and values are taught through our everyday lives as we honor and remember the Seven Generations: the three generations that come before us, the three generations that will come after us, and those we walk with today.

Kiisheelumukweengw
key-shall-ah-MOW-kwang
(Creator/the one who creates through thought)

WELCOME TO NANTICOKE INDIAN COUNTRY

Let's learn all about powwow and how to talk about what we see and hear there.

Haaw ha!
hauw hah
(Let's go!)

Piintiikeeshimowaak
peen-tee-kesh-ih-mo-WOK
(It's time for Grand Entry.)

Oonkuntuwaak
oon-kun-duh-WOK
(Blessing)

Nukantow
nuh-KUN-dow
(to sing)

Nukantomun
nuh-KUN-dow-mun
(we sing)

In loving memory of Katie Richardson
@Kim Richardson

Kuntkee
kunt-KAY
(to dance)

Nukuntkeemun
nuh-kunt-KAY-mun
(we dance)

Poohunik
POE-hun-ick
(drum)

Kunoontam ha poohunikans?
cuh-NOAN-tam hah poe-HUH-nick-cons
(Do you hear the drums?)

Poohunik kikun ahkiyii wumooshunapiyih
POE-hun-ick KICK-un ah*-KEY-e wuh-mush-un-AH-pee-yee
(The drum is the heartbeat of Mother Earth.)

Drumbeat

On the day of your birth we wrapped you, sweet baby, in a blanket, then placed you in your mother's arms. You drew in her scent and recognized your mother's **wumooshunapiyih** (heartbeat). And you, sweet baby, knew you were safe once again.

Your father held you, sweet baby, against his chest, and your heart began to beat with his. Your grandmother would sing to you, sweet baby, and you learned the rhythm of her heartbeat and songs.

Your grandfather would hold you, sweet baby, and you would listen to the beat of his heart as he patted your back. The rhythm of the heartbeat of our **Kikun Ahkiyii** (Our Earth Mother). Grandfather was teaching without words, the voice of the drum's heartbeat, sweet baby, the first time he held you in his arms.

Sweet baby, you will carry on the tradition. One day you will be a **Kiikaay** (Elder) who will teach little ones the way of the drum. The heartbeat of the drum sings out to **Kiisheelumukweengw** (the One who creates through thought). The heartbeat of our Earth Mother sings out her song to all living beings.

wumooshunapiyih
wuh-mush-un-AH-pee-yee
(heartbeat)

Kikun Ahkiyii
KICK-un ah*KEY-e
(Our Mother Earth)

Kiikaay
Key-kye
(Elder)

Kiisheelumukweengw
key-shall-ah-MOW-kwang
(Creator/
One who creates through thought)

Wiseekunus
wiss-EH-kun-us
(shawl)

Wiseekunusas
wiss-eh-KUN-us-sus
(shawls)

Miikw
ME-kw
(feather)

Miikwunak
ME-qun-uk
(feathers)

Eeweeshihik
eh-WESH-ih-hick
(a fan)

Eeweeshihikans
eh-wesh-ih-HICK-ahns
(fans)

Mahkus
MOH*-kuhs
(moccasin)

Mahkusuns
MOH*kuh-suns
(moccasins)

Maantsaap
MUN-sop
(bead)

Maantsaapiyak
mun-SOP-pee-ahk
(beads)

Soohkwutahas
SOH*-kwuh-tuh-hus
(succotash)

Salaapw
sa-LAP-w
(frybread)

Nuwiinkiitaam soohkwutahas waak salaapw
nuh-win-KEY-tahm SOH*-kwuh-tuh-hus wok   sa-LAP-w
(I like to eat succotash and frybread.)

Giveaway

When we want to celebrate an accomplishment or milestone in our own lives or in a family member's life, we hold a giveaway; for example: a wedding, birthday, graduation, or other occasion.

This is very different from celebrations you may know where the "honored" person expects or receives gifts from their guests.

At a giveaway ceremony, we give gifts to honor individuals who have helped and encouraged us on our journey.

That person or family who is the gift-giver may hold an honor dance and host a giveaway to acknowledge relatives and friends who helped them along the way.

That person or family may sometimes give gifts to all the guests present. It is with great respect that one gives to honor a relative. In doing so, that person is honored in the eyes of the community.

One gives when one seemingly has nothing to give. What matters is not what we have but what we are willing to offer to others.

Miiluwaak
me-lu-WOK
(gift)

Miiluwaakans
me-lu-WOK-ahns
(gifts)

Mat Haashii (Never Again)

Mat nuwaaniskeewinaanap
maht   nuh-one-ees-kay-wih-NAH-naap
We have not been forgotten.

Kihchi manitow numiilkwun nutiikiitoowaakanun
GIT-chee MAN-ih-toe   nuh-MIL-kwun   nuh-tee-key-toe-WOK-in-un
Gitchi Manitou gifted us our Tribal Tongue.

Mat nuwaaniskeewinaanap
maht   nuh-one-ees-kay-wih-NAH-naap
We have not been forgotten.

Kiikaayoomunaaniinkaa noontamuneewaa nutiikiitowaakanun
KEY-kye-you-mun-a-NEEN-ka non-tahn-mun-EH-wa   nuh-tee-key-toe-WOK-in-un
Our Ancestors hear our Tribal Tongue.

Wushoonuwaawah nukantowaawah
wuh-show-nuh-WA-wa   nuh-cone-tuh-WA-wa
Their hearts sing out.

Matach nooniwun nutiikiitowaakanun
mah-TOUCH NO-nee-one   nuh-tee-key-toe-WOK-in-un
We will not forget our Tribal Tongue.

Nutiikiitowusinaanach wunchii nushoonunaanas
nuh-tee-key-toe-wuh-SIH-nuch ONE-chee no-show-nuh-NAH-nuss
We will speak from our heart.

Ntahkeekimaanaanach miyaawaa ahanhookwii kishiikichik
GAH*-kay-key-ma-NAH-nuch   me-YAW-wa   ah-HAN-oh-kwee   key-SEE-kih-chick
We will teach our Tribal Tongue to the Seven Generations.

Mat haashii ahteewii taamsee mat noontamukwoowii nutiikiitowaakanun
maht HA-shee ah-TAY-we   TOM-see   maht non-tom-muh-KWOH-we nuh-tee-key-toe-WOK-in-un
Never will our Tribal Tongue be silenced again.

Sponsors

- Michael Apotheker
- Patric and Meredith Baumann
- Joanne Caputo and Michael Fleishman
- Terry and Deborah Forsythe
- John B. Grymes
- Dr. Howard R. Hall
- Dr. Jeanie M. Hall
- Randy Hall
- Gilbert and Linda Harmon
- Nikita D. Harmon
- Tonoa Harmon
- Herman W. Jackson
- Chief Avery "Leaving Tracks" Johnson
- Gail Johnson
- Bishop Peggy Johnson
- Jennifer Kerby and Brent Apotheker
- John and Tammy Lindberg
- Marion and Hugh Montague (In Memory of Gabriel)
- Megan E. Oates
- Sean Oates
- Taunya Oates
- Travis and Kate Oates
- Ragghi Rain
- Nancy O. Stanley
- Baltimore Washington Annual Conference
- Beacon Unitarian Universalist Church
- Camp Arrowhead
- Delaware District, Peninsula-Delaware Annual Conference (c/o Rev. Joseph Archie)
- Eastern Pennyslvania CoNAM
- Harmony United Methodist Church (In Honor of Rev. Charlotte Nichols)
- Morning Sky Initiative
- Mountain Sky Annual Conference
- Nanticoke Indian Association, Inc.
- Native American International Caucus
- Northeast Jurisdictional Native American Ministries Committee
- Peninsula-Delaware CoNAM
- UMC General Commission on Race and Religion (GCORR)
- UMC General Board of Global Ministries

For more information about the Nanticoke Language Project, please check out our website at www.nanticokelanguage.org

www.ingramcontent.com/pod-product-compliance
Lightning Source LLC
Chambersburg PA
CBHW060939170426
43194CB00027B/2999